Bach for Catholics

using chorales in the liturgy

 Edward Schaefer

The Pastoral Press
Washington, DC

Acknowledgments

Grateful acknowledgment is given to the following owners of copyright who have generously granted permission for inclusion of material in this booklet:

William Bates, for the Appendix extracted from his "An Index to the Organ Works of J.S. Bach," *The Diapason* 76 (June 1985) 9-13;

G. Schirmer, Inc., for the chorale tune *Herr Gott, dich loben wir,* as reprinted from *Johann Sebastian Bach: Complete Organ Works,* Edouard Nies-Berger and Albert Schweitzer, eds., vol. 6 (1954) 4.

Cambridge University Press, for all the remaining chorale tunes, except "St. Anne," as reprinted from Peter Williams, *The Organ Music of J. S. Bach,* vol. 2 (1980);

C. F. Peters Corporation, for the levels of difficulty assigned to the organ works discussed herein and other excerpts from Hermann Keller, *The Organ Works of J. S. Bach: A Contribution to Their History, Form, Interpretation and Performance* (1967), translated by Helen Hewitt;

Abbey St.-Pierre de Solesmes, for the chant melodies reprinted from *Antiphonale Monasticum* (1934), *Graduale Romanum* (1974), *Liber Antiphonarius* (in preparation), and *Liber Hymnarius* (1983).

ISBN: 0-912405-36-8

The Pastoral Press
225 Sheridan Street, NW
Washington, D.C. 20011
(202) 723-1254

The Pastoral Press is the publication division of the National Association of Pastoral Musicians, a membership organization of musicians and clergy dedicated to fostering the art of musical liturgy.

Printed in the United States of America

Contents

Introduction

Purpose

Musicians working in Catholic churches too often shy away from the chorale-based organ works of J.S. Bach. At first glance, it appears that most of the chorale tunes employed in these works are unfamiliar and unrelated to melodies sung in Catholic celebrations. However, a closer examination will reveal that a number of these chorales are more familiar and indeed more relevant to Catholic usage than at first might be supposed.

With the increased use of vernacular singing in the Catholic Church during the last twenty-five years, several of the chorales set by Bach have found their way into contemporary Catholic hymnals. Among these chorales are a few which are commonly known by names different from the titles given them in Bach's organ works. For example, the tune Bach employs in his settings of *Valet will ich dir geben* is known to most Catholic musicians as "St. Theodulph." Likewise, in the last of the *Schübler Chorales,* that is, the *Kommst du nun Jesu, vom Himmel herunter,* Bach uses a variant of the melody more commonly known as *Lobe den Herren.*

Also, a number of chorales which appear in Bach's organ works are adaptations of chant melodies which are sung— even if infrequently—in some Catholic churches today. These chants are representative of an important part of the heritage of the church, and the use of Bach's organ works which employ these melodies, or adaptations of them, is one way of preserving this heritage.

Thus, because a number of Bach's chorale-based organ works contain melodies which are either being sung with increased frequency in Catholic churches or are variants of chants, these compositions do indeed have a place in Catholic liturgy today. It is hoped that this booklet will encourage musicians serving in Catholic churches to make greater use of them.

Contents

This booklet contains all the chorales for which Bach provided organ settings and which either appear in at least one of a selected number of hymnals or have their roots in chant melodies. With regard to those chorales which are based on chants, the chants themselves are also identified, as are hymnals and other resources that contain them.

The hymnals selected for this survey include those deemed to be the more prominent ones currently used in the Catholic churches of the United States and Canada. These include *Catholic Book of Worship II*,[1] *Hymns, Psalms and Spiritual Canticles*,[2] *People's Mass Book*,[3] *Worship II*,[4] and *Worship*, 3rd edition.[5]

The Bach settings of the chorales catalogued in this work are also identified and classified according to level of difficulty.[6] Finally, suggestions are given for the use of both the chorales and organ settings.[7]

Organization

This work is divided into two main parts.

I. Chorales Appearing in Selected Catholic Hymnals
II. Chant-Based Chorales

In each section the chorales are catalogued in alphabetical order. After the name of each chorale is given, the tune itself appears. This is followed by a listing of the hymnals in which the melody can be found, an enumeration of the Bach organ works which use the tune, an indication of the level of difficulty of each of these works, and suggestions for the liturgical use of both the chorale and the organ works based on it. In Part II the chants upon which the chorales are based are also identified, as are hymnals and other resources which contain them.

Also included is a Liturgical Index which arranges the chorales discussed in this booklet according to appropriate usage during the year. An Appendix locates where the organ chorales catalogued in the body of the booklet may be found in the various modern performing editions of Bach's organ works.

Using This Booklet

The most efficient way to use this booklet is to begin with the Liturgical Index which lists all the chorales discussed. The listing gives various liturgical occasions for which the chorales are suitable. By referring to the Index first it becomes easy to find quickly those chorales which are appropriate for various liturgies being planned. Once a given chorale has been selected for possible use, it can be studied more carefully in the body of the work.

Abbreviations

Hymnals

CBW II - *Catholic Book of Worship II* (Ottawa: Canadian Conference of Catholic Bishops; and Toronto: Gordon V. Thompson, Ltd., 1980).

HPSC - *Hymns, Psalms and Spiritual Canticles*, rev. ed. (Belmont, MA: BACS Publishing Co., 1983).

PMB - *People's Mass Book*, rev. ed. (Schiller Park, IL: World Library Publications, 1984).

WII - *Worship II* (Chicago: G.I.A. Publications, 1975).

WIII - *Worship*, 3rd edition (Chicago: G.I.A. Publications, 1986).

Organic Works

BWV — *Bach-Werke-Verzeichnis* (Schmeider, Wolfgang, comp., *Thematisch-systematisches Verzeichnis der musicalischen Werke von Johann Sebastian Bach.* Leipzig: Breitkopf & Härtel, 1950). Schmeider's work is the standard catalogue of Bach's works.

(C) — Part of the collection *Clavier-Übung III.*

(OB) — Part of the collection *Orgelbüchlein.*

(S) — Part of the collection known as the *Schübler Chorales.*

(E) — Technically an easy work.

(MD) — Technically a work of medium difficulty.

(D) — Technically a difficult work.

(VD) — Technically a very difficult work.

Chant Sources

AM — *Antiphonale Monasticum pro Diurnis Horis* (Tournai: Desclée, 1934).

GR — *Graduale Sacrosanctae Romanae Ecclesiae de Tempore et de Sanctis* (Tournai: Desclée, 1974).

LA — *Liber Antiphonarius* (Solesmes: Les Éditions de Solesmes, in preparation).

LH — *Liber Hymnarius* (Solesmes: Les Éditions de Solesmes, 1983).

Bach
for Catholics

using chorales
in
the liturgy

PART I

CHORALES APPEARING IN
SELECTED
CATHOLIC HYMNALS

I
Ein' feste Burg

¹535

Hymnals: CBW II 641; HPSC 100; PMB 145; WII 2, 3; WIII 575, 576, 616

Organ Work: BWV 720 (D)

Recent efforts in ecumenism have seen this chorale drop one of its historic roles, that of a "battle cry" for the Reformed Churches. This should help Catholics make more frequent use of Luther's paraphrase of Psalm 46.

The lectionary assigns Psalm 46 only to the Tuesday of the Fourth Week of Lent,[8] but the chorale was also traditionally sung on the Third Sunday of this season. It appears in Bach's Cantata 80a, written for this Sunday.[9] The use of this chorale and Bach's organ setting of it on the First Sunday of Lent, Year A, when the gospel concerns the temptations of Christ, might be an appropriate way to recognize its traditional Lenten role while maintaining sensitivity to the themes of the lectionary.

II
Herzlich tut mich verlangen
or
Ach Herr, mich armen Sünder

Hymnals: CBW II 491; HPSC 248; PMB 50; WII
              211; WIII 434, 755

Organ Works: BWV 727 (E); BWV 742 (E)

It is fortunate that Bach left at least two organ settings of the "Passion Chorale" and perhaps even more so since they are virtually devoid of technical difficulties. Congregations should have the opportunity every Lent to sing this chorale and to hear at least one of Bach's organ settings.

III
In dir ist Freude

Witt 1715

Hymnals: WII 139

Organ Work   BWV 615 (OB 17, D)

The present form of *In dir ist Freude* demonstrates an evolutionary process still common today, that of placing a sacred text to a tune originally associated with a secular one. The melody of this chorale was first set with a ballett text.[10]

Bach's setting of "In Thee Is Gladness" falls in the New Year's section of the *Orgelbüchlein*. However, in the present liturgical calendar New Year's Day, the Octave of Christmas, is celebrated as a Marian feast, as it was in the early centuries of the church. The sentiment of this chorale suggests that it would be more appropriate for liturgies in which healing is emphasized, for example, funerals, celebrations of reconciliation, and rites of anointing the sick.

IV
In dulci jubilo

BWV 368

Hymnals: CBW II 465; HPSC 195; PMB 33;
                  WWII 105; WIII 391

Organ Works: BWV 608 (OB 10, D); BWV 729, 729a
                  (E); BWV 751 (D)

The original text of this delightful Christmas carol demonstrates a tradition of combining Latin and vernacular languages.[11] Bach was generous enough to provide this chorale with organ settings for varying levels of difficulty, thus denying no one the opportunity of participating in the "sweet joy" of Christmas.

V
Jesu, meine Freude

Hymnals: HPSC 198

Organ Works: BWV 610 (OB 12, MD); BWV 713, 713a (MD); BWV 743 (E); BWV Anhang 76 (E); BWV 1105 (E)

Bach used the chorale *Jesu, meine Freude* in cantatas for the seasons of Christmas and Epiphany and for other occasions throughout the liturgical year. His organ setting in the *Orgelbüchlein* appears in the Christmas section of the collection. Yet Williams comments that "it is not difficult to hear in the *Orgelbüchlein* setting a 'fervent longing' relevant to Advent rather than Christmas."[12] Indeed, this chorale and Bach's organ settings of it lend themselves to a wide range of applications.

VI
Kommst du nun, Jesu, vom Himmel herunter

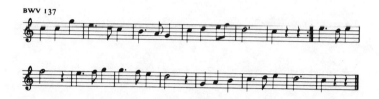

BWV 137

Hymnals: CBW II 652; HPSC 283, 284; PMB 122; WII 231; WIII 547

Organ Work: BWV 650 (S6 MD)

English-speaking Christians enjoy a variant of this melody in the hymn "Praise to the Lord, the Almighty." The sparkling organ setting, although somewhat demanding technically, is certainly a rewarding part of any organist's repertoire—for both the organist and the congregation.

VII
Liebster Jesu, wir sind hier

Hymnals: CBW II 559; HPSC 355; PMB 105; WIII 513

Organ Works: BWV 633 (OB 35b, MD); BWV 634 (OB 35a, MD); BWV 706/1, 706/2 (E); BWV 730 (MD); BWV 731 (MD); BWV 734 (MD)

Today this enduring tune is matched with a variety of texts. James Quinn's "Word of God, Come Down on Earth" is favored in Catholic hymnals, and it seems to be sung most often as an Advent hymn. However, its use for other occasions should not be overlooked.

VIII
Nun danket alle Gott

BWV 252

Hymnals: CBW II 674; HPSC 230, 231; PMB 130; WII 189; WIII 560

Organ Work: BWV 657, 657a (L7, D)

It is the very nature of Christians to give thanks. Thus this hymn, and its organ setting by Bach, should find regular use throughout the year.

IX
St. Anne

Hymnals: CBW II 640; HPSC 241, 242; PMB 128; WII 203; WIII 579

Organ Work   BWV 552 (C, D-VD)

    The hymn "O God, Our Help in Ages Past," a paraphrase of Psalm 90, is most commonly associated with the "St. Anne" melody. The lectionary appoints Psalm 90 to several specific days,[13] but the hymn would be appropriate for any liturgies in which trust in and dependency upon God are central themes, for example, during funerals.

    BWV 552 consists of a prelude and a fugue. The reference to "St. Anne" occurs in the fugue which is by far the easier of the two pieces. It stands well by itself and could be played without the prelude with no loss of integrity to the work or the organist.

X
Valet will ich dir geben

Hymnals:　　　　　CBW II 486; HPSC 105; PMB 41; WII
　　　　　　　　　9; WIII 428, 706

Organ Works:　　　BWV 735, 735a (MD); BWV 736/1 (D);
　　　　　　　　　BWV 736/2 (E)

Most Catholics will recognize this melody as "All Glory Laud and Honor" ("St. Theodulph"), most often sung during the Palm Sunday procession which recalls Christ's triumphal entry into Jerusalem. This same Palm Sunday liturgy, however, only moments later focuses intensely on Christ's imminent suffering and death with the reading of the passion. It is a fascinating twist of fate that the text Bach associated with this chorale tune translates "I shall say farewell to you, O wicked, false world..."[14] With a melody sung to recall Christ's triumphal entry into Jerusalem and a historical association with a text looking toward imminent death, perhaps there is no other work that more successfully ties together the seemingly disparate themes of Palm Sunday than Bach settings of *Valet will ich dir geben*.

XI
Vater unser im Himmelreich

1539

Hymnals: WII 198

Organ Works: BWV 636 (OB37, E); BWV 682 (C14,
                D); BWV 683, 683a (C15, MD); BWV
                737 (E); BWV 760 (E); BWV 761 (MD);
                BWV 762 (MD)

Luther set a versified form of the Lord's Prayer to this
tune. Bach, in turn, provided several organ settings of
varying levels of difficulty. At least one of them should find
its way into the repertoire of every organist.

XII
Vom Himmel hoch, da komm' ich her

1539

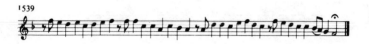

Hymnals: WII 89; WIII 388

Organ Works: BWV 606 (OB8, MD); BWV 700 (E);
                 BWV 701 (D); BWV 738, 738a (MD);
                 BWV 769, 769a (D)

Luther provided both the text and the tune of this now familiar Christmas hymn.[15] The melody appears not only in several organ settings by Bach but also in his *Christmas Oratorio*.

XIII
Wachet auf, ruft uns die Stimme

BWV 140, final chorale (simplified)

Hymnals: CBW II 451; HPSC 338; PMB 10; WII 291; WIII 371

Organ Work: BWV 645 (S1, MD)

Bach's organ setting of *Wachet auf,* transcribed from Cantata 140, has become one of his more famous organ works. The text of the chorale refers to Matthew 25:1-13. Thus the chorale and the organ setting are specifically appropriate to the Thirty-Second Sunday of the Year, Year A, one of the last Sundays of the liturgical year. However, these works would also be suitable for use in Advent, since the message of these verses in Matthew, "Be watchful and ready," also permeates the readings of this season.

15

XIV
Wer nur den lieben Gott lässt walten

G. Neumark 1657

BWV 179

Hymnals: HPSC 191

Organ Works: BWV 642 (OB43, MD); BWV 647 (S3, MD); BWV 690/1, 690/2 (E); BWV 691, 691a (E)

    The text most often associated with this tune, "If Thou but Suffer God to Guide Thee," is based on Psalm 55:2. Although this psalm is proper to the feast of the Triumph of the Holy Cross, the sentiment of the text would also make it appropriate for reconciliation liturgies, funerals, and other celebrations in which emphasis is placed on trust in the everlasting love and care of God.

XV
Wie schön leuchtet der Morgenstern

BWV 172

Hymnals: CBW II 680; HPSC 256; WII 119; WIII
             389, 390

Organ Works: BWV 739 (MD); BWV 763 (MD)

The melody *Wie schön leuchtet* seems to have been attached
to several texts, even in Bach's time. Bach employed the
tune in six cantatas for different feasts and seasons
throughout the liturgical year.[16] *The Lutheran Hymnal* (1941)
uses the melody for seven different texts,[17] and the
Lutheran Book of Worship (1978) uses it for five.[18] Of the three
Catholic hymnals in which *Wie schön leuchtet* appears, no two
attach it to identical texts. Ostensibly, the appropriate
application of Bach's settings of this tune will depend on
the text that a particular congregation associates with it.

PART II
CHANT-BASED CHORALES

XVI
Allein Gott in der Höh' sei Ehr'

Vopelius 1682

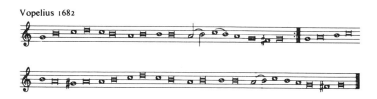

Chant Source: *Gloria*, Mass I GR 712

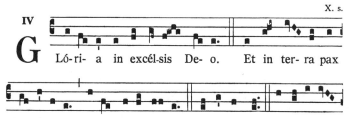

X. s.

Ló-ri- a in excél-sis De- o.   Et in ter- ra pax

ho-mí-ni-bus bonae vo-luntá- tis. Laudámus te. Be-ne-dí-ci-

(ed. Abbey St.-Pierre de Solesmes)

Hymnals, Chant: None

Hymnals, Chorale: WIII 527

Organ Works: BWV 662, 662a (112, MD); BWV 663,
                  663a (L13, MD); BWV 664, 664a, 664b
                  (L14, D); BWV 675 (C7, MD); BWV
                  676, 676a (C8, D); BWV 677 (C9, MD);
                  BWV 711 (D); BWV 715 (MD); BWV
                  716 (E); BWV 717 (MD); BWV 771 (E)

Mass I was traditionally reserved for use on Easter, and the text of the *Gloria* begins with the acclamation of the angels on Christmas. This suggests that any festive occasion, that is, any occasion on which the *Gloria* is sung, would be appropriate for any of the works based on this melody.

XVII
Christ lag in Todesbanden

BWV 277

and
Christ ist erstanden

Chant Source: *Victimae paschali laudes* GR 198

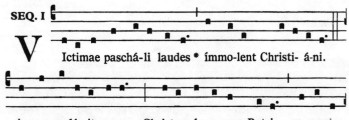

SEQ. I

Victimae paschá-li laudes * ímmo-lent Christi- á-ni.

Agnus re-démit oves : Christus ínno-cens Patri   re-conci-

(ed. Abbey St.-Pierre de Solesmes)

Hymnal, Chant: HPSC 342; WII 290; WIII 461

Hymnal, Chorales: (*Christ lag in Todesbanden*) WII 45;
                  (*Christ ist erstanden*) PMB 75; CBWII 498

Organ Works: (*Christ lag in Todesbanden*) BWV 625
                (OB27, E); BWV 695/1, 695/1a, 695/2
                (E); BWV 718 (E); BWV Anhang 171
                (E); (*Christ ist erstanden*) BWV 627
                (OB29, D); BWV 746 (E)

Every Catholic should know this chant! It is the sequence for the Mass of Easter, one of the four sequences preserved for use in the Mass by the Council of Trent. The venerable tradition of singing the Easter sequence, either in Latin or in English,[19] should be a high priority in the choir's preparation for Easter. Similarly, at least one of Bach's settings of the chorale versions should be heard every Easter.

XVIII
Christum wir sollen loben schon
or
Was fürchtst du, Feind Herodes sehr'

Chant Sources: *A solus ortu(s) cardine* LH 22
or
Hostis Herodes impie AM 288

(ed. Abbey St.-Pierre de Solesmes)

Hymnals, Chant: None

Hymnals, Chorale: None

Organ Works: BWV 611 (OB13, MD); BWV 969
                  (MD)

This chant melody was sung with either a Christmas (*A solis ortu[s] cardine*) or Epiphany (*Hostis Herodes impie*) text. The Christmas text served as the hymn for lauds of Christmas, and the Epiphany text for the hymn of first vespers of Epiphany, the feast which closes the Christmas season. In Bach's settings of the chorale version of the chant, he gives alternate titles to BWV 969, one for Christmas (*Christum wir sollen loben schon*) and the other for Epiphany (*Was fürchtst du, Feind Herodes sehr'*), but only offers the Christmas title for the *Orgelbüchlein* setting, BWV 611. Nonetheless, both pieces are well-suited for use throughout the Christmas season.

XIX
Herr Gott, dich loben wir

Chant Source: *Te Deum laudamus* (tonus simplex) GR
841, LH 530

E De- um laudá-mus : • te Dómi-num confi-té-mur.

Te aetérnum Patrem omnis terra ve-ne-rá-tur. Ti-bi   omnes

(ed. Abbey St.-Pierre de Solesmes)

Hymnals, Chant: CBWII 631; HPSC 361 (variant)

The following hymnals contain translations of the text set to a different
tune: HPSC 180; PMB 127; WII 117;
WIII 524.

Hymnals, Chorale: None

Organ Work: BWV 725 (MD)

The translated text of the *Te Deum*, "Holy God, We Praise
Thy Name," is undoubtedly more familiar than the
Gregorian melody to most Catholics. Although the hymn
is proper to the office of readings (formerly, matins), it
was—and certainly still may be—employed "for general
use in public and solemn thanksgiving."[20]

XX
Komm, Gott Schöpfer, heiliger Geist

Anon 1535

Chant Source: *Veni Creator Spiritus* GR 848, LH 90

H.VIII

V E·ni, cre· á·tor Spí·ri·tus, mentes tu·ó·rum ví·si·

ta, imple su·pérna grá·ti· a, quæ tu cre· ásti, péctora.

(ed. Abbey St.-Pierre de Solesmes)

Hymnals, Chant: WII 205, 289; CBWII 514, 515; WIII 475, 479

The following hymnals contain translations of the text set to a different tune: WII 50; HPSC 340; PMB 89; CBWII 516; WII 482.

Hymnals, Chorale: None

Organ Works: BWV 631, 631a (OB33, E); BWV 667, 667a, 667b (L17, MD)

Young organists might find it enlightening, perhaps even inspiring, to know that many older Catholics can still recall the great Pentecost hymn *Veni Creator Spiritus*, which in monastic observances was traditionally sung at lauds. Even those Catholics unfamiliar with the tune will most certainly recognize the translated text "Come, Holy

Ghost." Thus, this is a chant which probably could be (re)introduced to parishes without great difficulty. The Bach settings of the chorale version might be especially useful in such efforts, since the chorale form closely adheres to its chant predecessor, and the long-note *cantifirmi* Bach employs in his settings should be easily recognized by congregations.

In addition to the obvious appropriateness of these works for Pentecost, they could also be played on occasions when the votive Mass of the Holy Spirit is celebrated.

XXI
Kyrie, Gott heiliger Geist
and
Kyrie, Gott Vater in Ewigkeit
and
Christe, aller Welt Trost

Vopelius 1682

Chant Source: *Kyrie (Summum bonum) fons bonitatis,* Mass
II GR 715

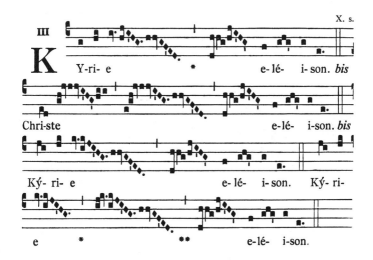

(ed. Abbey St.-Pierre de Solesmes)

Hymnals, Chant: None

Hymnals, Chorale: None

Organ Works: (*Kyrie, Gott heiliger Geist*) BWV 671 (C3,
                  MD); BWV 674 (C6, MD); (*Kyrie, Gott
                  Vater*) BWV 669 (C1, MD); BWV 672
                  (C4, MD); (*Christe, aller Welt*) BWV 670
                  (C2, MD); BWV 673 (C5, MD)

The chants of Mass II, of which this *Kyrie* is a part, have
not maintained the level of popularity in the twentieth
century enjoyed by some of the other chants of the
Gradual, for example, the *Sanctus* of Mass XVIII or *Credo I*.
Nonetheless, the works of Bach based on the chorale
version of this chant should not be overlooked. For each
chorale there are two settings. The first is a large chorale
motet; the second is a short fughetta. The fughettas are
easier to play and perhaps would be more appropriate for
penitential seasons and liturgies when special emphasis is
placed on the *Kyrie*.

The large, and considerably more ambitious, settings
would be more suitable for feast days. Keller maintains
that these arrangements were "intended for major
feasts,"[21] and Mass II was generally reserved for feasts of
the first class.[22]

XXII
Lob sei dem allmächtigen Gott

1531

Chant Source: *Conditor (Creator) alme siderum* LH 3

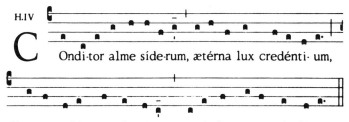

Ondi-tor alme síde-rum, ætérna lux credénti- um,

Christe, redémptor ómni- um, exáudi preces súpplicum.

(ed. Abbey St.-Pierre de Solesmes)

Hymnals, Chant: CBWII 539; HPSC 147, 260; PMB 3, 4, 5; WII 65; WIII 368

Hymnals, Chorale: None

Organ Works: BWV 602 (OB4, MD); BWV 704 (E)

The chant *Conditor (Creator) alme siderum* was traditionally sung as the hymn of vespers during Advent. Today the tune continues to be associated with any of several translations of the Latin text, for example, "Dear Maker of the Starry Skies."

In HPSC, however, the tune also appears with the text by Aquinas, "O Saving Victim Op'ning Wide," which is most often sung during exposition and adoration of the blessed sacrament. The melody is especially appropriate for this text when eucharistic devotions are connected with vespers during Advent. The organ works using the chorale form of the tune are well-suited to these and other Advent celebrations.

31

XXIII
Meine Seele erhebt den Herren
or
Magnificat

BWV 324

Chant Source   *Tonus "Peregrinus"* LA

Sic incí·pi·tur, et sic flécti·tur, † et sic me·di· á·   tur;*

Atque sic fi·ní·   tur.

(ed. St.-Pierre de Solesmes)

Hymnals, Chant: None

Hymnals, Chorale: None

Organ Works: BWV 648 (S4, MD); BWV 733 (D)

Williams remarks that "the *Magnificat* is the only canticle or psalm tone to keep intact its original Gregorian melody."[23] Thus, the close affinity between this psalm tone and the *Magnificat* suggests that the Bach settings be reserved for Masses on Marian feasts, especially the feasts of the Visitation (31 May) and the Assumption (15 August), the Third Sunday of Advent, Year B, the various weekdays when this text is prescribed,[24] and, of course, celebrations of evening prayer at any time.

XXIV
Nun komm, der Heiden Heiland

BWV 36

Chant Source: *Veni Redemptor gentium* LH 11

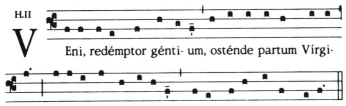

H.II

V Eni, redémptor génti- um, osténde partum Vírgi-

nis; mi·ré·tur omne sǽculum : ta·lis decet partus De·um.

(ed. Abbey St.-Pierre de Solesmes)

Hymnals, Chant: None

Hymnals, Chorale: WII 241

Organ Works: BWV 599 (OB1, E); BWV 659, 659a (L9, MD); BWV 660, 660a, 660b (L10, MD); BWV 661, 661a (L11, MD); BWV 699 (E)

Surprisingly, the chant form of this tune does not appear in any of the chant books commonly employed in the twentieth century.[25] However, Luther was well-acquainted with Ambrose's Advent hymn, since the chorale form of this melody appears with his German translation in many seventeenth century Lutheran hymnbooks as "the chief hymn of the four Sundays in Advent."[26] The chorale appears in WII with a translation of the Advent text "Savior of the Nations, Come." Organ works based on this tune certainly continue to be excellent additions to the liturgies of Advent.

XXV
Wir glauben all' an einen Gott

BWV 437

Chant Source: *Credo IV* GR 776

Re-do   in unum De- um, Patrem omni-pot- én- tem,

factó-rem cae-li   et ter- rae,   vi- si- bí- li- um ómni- um, et in-

(ed. Abbey St.-Pierre de Solesmes)

Hymnals, Chant: None

Hymnals, Chorale: None

Organ Works: BWV 680 (C12, MD); BWV 681 (C13,
                 MD); BWV 740 (D); BWV 765 (MD);
                 BWV 1098 (E)

Credo IV was commonly called *Credo Cardinale* during the sixteenth and seventeenth centuries. The practice of singing this melody on the "principal solemnities of the year"[27] may suggest the use of these organ chorales on similar occasions today.

Notes

Introduction

1. *Catholic Book of Worship II* (Ottawa: Canadian Conference of Catholic Bishops; Toronto: Gordon V. Thompson, Ltd., 1980).
2. *Hymns, Psalms and Spiritual Canticles,* rev. ed. (Belmont, MA: BACS Publishing Co., 1983).
3. *People's Mass Book,* rev. ed. (Schiller Park, IL: World Library Publications, 1984).
4. *Worship II* (Chicago: G.I.A. Publications, 1975).
5. *Worship,* 3rd edition (Chicago: G.I.A. Publications, 1986).
6. The indications of difficulty are those assigned by Hermann Keller in his book *The Organ Works of Bach: A Contribution to Their History, Form, Interpretation and Performance,* trans., Helen Hewitt (New York: C.F. Peters, 1967), i.e., for those pieces treated in this work. For works not discussed by Keller, the indications of difficulty are the opinions of the author.
7. The reader might also find useful Peter Williams' *The Organ Music of J.S. Bach,* 3 vols. (Cambridge: Cambridge Univ. Press, 1980-1984) for analyses of the organ pieces and Marilyn Kay Stulken's *Hymnal Companion to the Lutheran Book of Worship* (Philadelphia: Fortress Press, 1981) for detailed histories of the chorale melodies.

Part I

8. *Lectionary for Mass* (New York: Catholic Book Publishing Company, 1970) 352.
9. Williams, *The Organ Music of J.S. Bach,* vol. 2, 260.
10. The ballett was a lively song, characterized by a dance-like spirit and the use of nonsense syllables "fa la la" in a refrain. For the text of this ballett see Stulken, *Companion to the Lutheran Book of Worship* 557.
11. In this case the vernacular was German. For the first verse of the original macaronic text, see Stulken, *Companion to the Lutheran Book of Worship* 158.
12. Williams, *The Organ Music of J.S. Bach,* vol. 2, 36. The expression "fervent longing" is cited by Williams from P. Spitta, *Johann Sebastian Bach,* 2 vols. (Leipzig, 1873-1879), vol. 1, 590.
13. See *Lectionary,* "Index of Responsorial Psalms," 1116.
14. See Williams, *The Organ Music of J.S. Bach,* vol. 2, 281, for a full translation of verse one.
15. See Stulken, *Companion to the Lutheran Book of Worship,* 153-154.
16. See Williams, *The Organ Music of J.S. Bach,* vol. 2, 287.
17. *The Lutheran Hymnal* (St. Louis: Concordia Publishing House, 1941).
18. *Lutheran Book of Worship* (Minneapolis: Augsburg Publishing House; Philadelphia: Board of Publication, Lutheran Church in America, 1978).

19. For example, see Richard Proulx, *The Pilgrim* (Chicago: G.I.A. Publications, 1980) 7.

20. Peter Wagner, *Introduction to the Gregorian Melodies,* 2 ed., trans., Agnes Orme and E.G.P. Wyatt, Part I (London: Plainsong and Medieval Music Society); reprinted with a new introduction by Richard Crocker (New York: Da Capo Press, 1986) 151.

21. Keller, *The Organ Works of Bach* 271.

22. Wagner cites several traditional uses of the *Kyrie* outside of Mass, including Easter vespers. See his *Introduction to the Gregorian Melodies,* Part I, 64.

23. Williams, *The Organ Music of J.S. Bach,* vol. 2, 117.

24. See the various indices in the *Lectionary* 1102ff.

25. Its inclusion in the recent *Liber Hymnarius* is most welcome.

26. D. Gojowy, "Lied und Sonntag in Gesangbuchern der Bach-Zeit: Zur Frage des 'Detempore' bei Choralen in Bachs Kantaten," *Bach-Jahrbuch* 58 (1972), 24–60; cited by Williams, *The Organ Music of J.S. Bach,* vol. 2, 15.

27. Donald Marcase, "Adriano Banchieri. *L'Organo suonarino*: Translation, Transcription and Commentary" (Ph.D. Dissertation, Indiana University, 1970) 110.

Liturgical Index

Seasons and Feasts of the Liturgical Year

Rites of the Church

Reconciliation

Vespers (Evening Prayer)

Miscellaneous

See *Seasons and Feasts of the Liturgical Year*: Miscellaneous.

Liturgical Themes

Faith

Healing

See *Rites of the Church*: Anointing of the Sick; Funeral; Reconciliation

Prayer

Thanksgiving

See *Seasons and Feasts of the Liturgical Year*: Thanksgiving.

Trust

Miscellaneous

See *Seasons and Feasts of the Liturgical Year*: Miscellaneous.

Appendix

This Appendix is extracted from "An Index to the Organ Works of J. S. Bach" by William Bates[1] and is provided as a tool for locating modern performing editions of the Bach works discussed elsewhere in this booklet.

Concerning This Appendix

All compositions are identified by title and BWV number (an alternate version or variant reading of a composition is indicated by a letter suffix). A single asterisk after the BWV number indicates that the given composition is preserved in an autograph manuscript, a double asterisk that the piece is preserved in a Bach-authorized print. Additional information identifies each piece that belongs to a Bach-compiled collection (for example, S5 = the fifth of the Schübler Chorales). German chorale titles have been spelled according to modern practice. When in a modern edition two versions of a composition are printed together—with one version being shown in regular type and the other, when it differs, by means of alternate notations—the version to which the alternate readings belong is identified by the placement of square brackets around the edition citation.[2] A plus sign placed after an edition indicates that only a portion of the given composition appears in that particular source.

Primary Modern Editions

BGA = Bach-Gesellschaft-Ausgabe (*Johann Sebastian Bachs Werke.* 47 vols. Leipzig: Breitkopf & Härtel, 1851-99, 1926; reprint ed., Ann Arbor, MI: J. W. Edwards, 1947).

Lo = Lohmann, Heinz (ed.). *Johann Sebastian Bach: Sämtliche Orgelwerke.* 10 vols. (EB 6581-6590). Wiesbaden: Breitkopf & Härtel, 1968-79.

NBA = Neue-Bach-Ausgabe (*Johann Sebastian Bach: Neue Ausgabe sämtliche Werke*. Series IV—Organ Works, 8 vols. to date. Kassel: Barenreiter, 1958—; softback offprints of the 8 volumes are available from the same publisher under the title *Johann Sebastian Bach: Orgelwerke/Organ Works* [BA 5171-5181]). In the present index some spaces in the NBA column have been left blank in order to facilitate the later inclusion of page citations from the as yet unpublished portions of the series.

Pe = Griepenkerl, F. C., and Roitzsch, Ferdinand (eds.). *Johann Sebastian Bachs Kompositionen für die Orgel*. 9 vols. (EP 240-247, 2067). Leipzig: C. F. Peters, 1844-52 (vols. 1-8), 1881 (vol. 9 added), 1904 (vol 9 rev. by Max Seiffert), 1950 (vol. 9 rev. [1940] by Hermann Keller); new, 8 volume edition in preparation (vol. 1 [EP 9940; ed. by Klaus Schubert, 1982] now available).

WS = Widor, Charles-Marie, and Schweitzer, Albert (eds.). *Johann Sebastian Bach: Complete Organ Works*. 8 vols. New York: G. Schirmer, 1912-13 (vols. 1-5; reprint ed., 1940-41); 1954-67 (vols. 6-8, edited by Edouard Nies-Berger and Albert Schweitzer).

Other Editions and Abbreviations

BB = Selected organ works of J. S. Bach, ed. by C. Boer (Amsterdam: Broekmans & Van Poppel).

BWV = Bach-Werke-Verzeichnis (Schmeider, Wolfgang, comp. *Thematische- systematisches Verzeichnis der musicalischen Werke von Johann Sebastian Bach*. Leipzig: Breitkopf & Härtel, 1950. An appendix ("Anhang") to Schmeider's catalogue lists works either questionably or erroneously attributed to Bach; only a few of these compositions are listed in the present index.

C   = *Clavier-Übung III* (chorale settings = BWV 669–689).

Coll.   = Collection.

CP   = Clark, Robert, and Peterson, John David, eds. *Johann Sebastian Bach: Orgelbüchlein.* St Louis: Concordia, 1984.

EOM   = Bach, Johann Sebastian. *Prelude, Trio and Fugue in B Flat for Organ.* Ed. Walter Emery. Early Organ Music, No. 12. London: Novello, 1959.

EP   = Edition Peters.

JCB   = Johann Christoph Bach (J. S. Bach's uncle).

JSB   = Johann Sebastian Bach.

K   = Bach, Johann Sebastian. *Complete Organ Works.* 9 vols. (Kalmus 3070–3078). New York: Edwin F. Kalmus, [1947]. Because this edition is a reprint of the 1881 Peters edition, the content of vol. 9 differs slightly from that of the Peters edition of 1950.

KB   = "Kritischer Bericht" (Critical Commentary) of NBA.

L   = "18" Leipzig chorales (BWV 651–668). Sometimes the last chorale, *Vor deinen Thron,* is not considered part of the collection.

ME   = Modern edition.

N   =   Bach, Johann Sebastian. *Organ Chorales from the Neumeister Collection*. Ed. Christoph Wolff. New Haven, CT: Yale University Press, 1985; and Kassel: Bärenreiter (BA 5181), 1985.

OB   =   *Orgel-Büchlein* (BWV 599–644).

S   =   Schübler Chorales (BWV 645–650).

SO   =   Stauffer, George. *The Organ Preludes of Johann Sebastian Bach*. Ann Arbor MI: UMI Research Press, 1980; paperback ed., 1984.

Composition	Coll.	Modern Editions				
		BGA	Lo	NBA	Pe	WS
Allein Gott in der Höh' sei Ehr' 662* (orn. sop.)	L12	25/2:122	7:131	2:67	6:26	8:56
(662a)		—	[7:131]	2:168	—	—
Allein Gott 663* (in G)	L13	25/2:125	7:136	2:72	6:22	8:60
(663a)³		25/2:180	[7:136]	2:172	6:100	—
Allein Gott 664* (trio)	L14	25/2:130	7:143	2:79	6:17	8:64
(664a)		25/2:183	7:183	[2:179]	6:97	—
(664b)		—	[7:183]	2:179	—	—
Allein Gott 675** (in F; man.-ped. arr. in Lo 8:160)	C7	3:197	8:26	4:30	6:10	7:72
Allein Gott 676** (6/8)	C8	3:199	8:28	4:33	6:12	7:74
(676a; by JSB?)		40:208	8:164	KB4:48	6:96	6:25
Allein Gott 677* (man.; in A)	C9	3:205	8:34	4:41	6:29	7:79
Allein Gott 711 (Johann Bernhard Bach?)		40:34	9:5	3:11	6:6	6:23
Allein Gott 715		40:44	9:8	3:14	9:45	6:1
Allein Gott 716 (by JSB?)		40:45	9:9		6:30	6:21
Allein Gott 717 (12/8)		40:47	9:11	3:8	6:8	6:27
Allein Gott 771 (Andreas Nicolaus Vetter?)		40:195	10:60			8:122+
Christ ist erstanden 627*	OB29	25/2:40	7:44	1:49	5:4	7:40
Christ ist erstanden 746 (J.C.F. Fischer?)		40:173	—		—	6:110+
Christ lag in Todesbanden 625*	OB27	25/2:38	7:42	1:46	5:7	7:38
Christ lag 695/1		40:10	9:15	3:20	6:43	6:34
[chorale] 695/2		40:12	9:17	3:22	6:45	6:2
(695/1a = arr.; by JSB?)		40:153	9:143	—	6:104	—

Composition	Coll.	Modern Editions				
		BGA	Lo	NBA	Pe	WS
Christ lag 718 (fantasy)		40:52	9:18	3:16	6:40	6:31
Christ lag Anhang 171 (Johann Pachelbel)		40:174	—		—	6:111+
Christe, aller Welt Trost 670**	C2	3:186	8:14	4:18	7:20	7:63
Christe, aller Welt Trost 673** (man.)	C5	3:194	8:23	4:28	7:27	7:70
Christum wir sollen loben schon 611*	OB13	25/2:15	7:18	1:20	5:8	7:15
Christum wir sollen 696 (or Was fürchtst du)		40:13	9:22	3:23	5:9	6:36
Ein' feste Burg ist unser Gott 720		40:57	9:32	3:24	6:58	6:41
Herr Gott, dich loben wir 725		40:66	9:47	3:36	6:65	6:4
Herzlich tut mich verlangen 727		40:73	9:57	3:46	5:30	6:54
Herzlich tut mich verlangen 742 (also in N; known also as Ach Herr, mich armen Sünder 742)		—	—		(K9:67)	—
In dir ist Freude 615*	OB17	25/2:20	7:23	1:27	5:36	7:20
In dulci jubilo 608*	OB10	25/2:12	7:14	1:16	5:38	7:12
In dulci jubilo 729		40:74	9:67	3:52	5:103	6:12
(729a)		40:158	9:148	3:50	—	6:11
In dulci jubilo 751 (Johann Michael Bach?)		—	9:69		9:50	6:59
Jesu, meine Freude 610*	OB12	25/2:14	7:17	1:19	5:34	7:14
Jesu, meine Freude 713		40:38	9:71	3:54	6:78	6:61
[chorale] Anhang 76		—	9:74	3:57	6:81	—
(713a in d; by JSB?)		40:155	—	—	6:110	—

Composition	Coll.	Modern Editions				
		BGA	Lo	NBA	Pe	WS
Jesu, meine Freude [incomplete] 753*4 (for harpsicord?)		40:163	—		5:112	6:64
Jesu, meine Freude 1105 (ME = N:38)		—	—		—	—
Komm, Gott Schöpfer heiliger Geist 631*	OB33	25/2:47	7:52	1:58	7:86/B	7:47
(631a)*	OB33	25/2:150	—	1:82	7:86/A	—
Komm, Gott Schöpfer heiliger Geist 667	L17	25/2:142	7:159	2:94	7:2	8:74
(667a; no ME currently available?)						
(667b)		—	7:194	2:194	—	—
Kommst du nun Jesu 650**	S6	25/2:74	8:118	1:98	7:16	8:12
Kyrie, Gott heiliger Geist 671**	C3	3:190	8:18	4:22	7:23	7:66
Kyrie, Gott heiliger Geist 674** (man.)	C6	3:196	8:24	4:29	7:28	7:71
Kyrie, Gott Vater 669**	C1	3:184	8:12	4:16	7:18	7:61
Kyrie, Gott Vater 672** (man.)	C4	3:194	8:22	4:27	7:26	7:69
Liebster Jesu wir sind hier 633* ("distinctus")	OB35b	25/2:50	7:55	1:61	5:40	7:50
Liebster Jesu 634*	OB35a	25/2:49	7:54	1:60	5:109	7:49
Liebster Jesu 706/1		40:25/1	9:76/1	3:59/1	5:39	6:14/1
[chorale] 706/2		40:25/2	9:76/2	3:59/2	5:39	6:14/2
Liebster Jesu 730 (in G)		40:76	9:77	3:60	5:105/1	6:67
Liebster Jesu 731 (orn. sop.)		40:77	9:78	3:61	5:105/2	6:68
Liebster Jesu 754 (not by JSB)		—	9:79	—	(K9:50)	—
Lob sei dem allmächtigen Gott 602*	OB4	25/2:13	7:5	1:7	5:40	7:5
Lob sei dem allmächtigen Gott 704		40:22	9:81	3:62	5:41	6:69

Composition	Coll.	Modern Editions				
		BGA	Lo	NBA	Pe	WS
Magnificat, Fuga sopra il 733 (or Meine Seele erhebt)		40:79	9:83	3:65	7:29	6:70
Meine Seele erhebt den Herren 648**	S4	25/2:70	8:112	1:94	7:33	8:8
Meine Seele erhebt 733 (see Magnificat 733)						
Nun danket alle Gott 657*	L7	25/2:108	7:111	2:46	7:34	8:44
(657a)[5]		—	[7:111]	—	—	—
Nun komm, der Heiden Heiland 599*	OB1	25/2:3	7:1	1:3	5:44	7:2
Nun komm, der Heiden Heiland 659*	L9	25/2:114	7:118	2:55	7:38	8:48
(659a)		25/2:172	[7:118]	2:157	7:92	—
Nun komm, der Heiden Heiland 660* (trio)	L10	25/2:116	7:122	2:59	7:40	8:50
(660a)*		25/2:174	[7:122]	2:160	7:93	—
(660b; not by JSB)		25/2:176	—	—	7:94	8:132
Nun komm, der Heiden Heiland 661* (c.f. in pedal)	L11	25/2:118	7:126	2:62	7:42	8:52
(661a)[6]		25/2:178	[7:126]	2:164	7:96	—
Nun komm, der Heiden Heiland 699		40:16	9:94	3:73	5:45	6:79
St. Anne (Fugue of Prelude and Fugue in E flat 522** in Clavier-Übung III)[7]		3:254	1:94 8:92	4:105	3:10	3:72
Valet will ich dir geben 735 (19th-cen. arr.?)		40:86	9:102	3:77	7:53	6:80
(735a)		40:161	9:150	3:81	7:100	—
Valet will ich 736/1 (c.f. in pedal)		40:90	9:106	3:84	7:56	6:84
[chorale] 736/2		—	9:110	3:89	—	—
Vater unser im Himmelreich 636*	OB37	25/2:52	7:58	1:64	5:52	7:52

Composition	Coll.	Modern Editions				
		BGA	Lo	NBA	Pe	WS
Vater unser 682**	C14	3:217	8:49	4:58	7:60	7:90
Vater unser 683** (man.)	C15	3:223	8:56	4:66	5:51	7:95
(683a; by JSB?)		—	8:166	KB4:51	5:109	—
Vater unser 737		40:96	9:111	3:90	7:66	6:88
Vater unser 760 (Georg Böhm)		40:183		—	—	6:116
Vater unser 761 (Georg Böhm)		40:184		—	—	6:117
Vater unser 762 (not by JSB)		—	9:112	9:54	9:90	—
Vom Himmel hoch da komm' ich her 606*	OB8	25/2:9	7:10	1:13	5:53	7:10
Vom Himmel hoch 700		40:17	9:114	3:92	7:68	6:94
Vom Himmel hoch 701 (fughetta)		40:19	9:116	3:96	7:67	6:92
Vom Himmel hoch 738 (12/8)		40:97	9:118	3:94	5:106	6:17
(738a)		40:159	9:153	3:94	—	6:16
Vom Himmel hoch 769** (Canonic Variations)		40:137	8:142	2:197	5:92	8:106
(769a)		—	8:126	2:98	—	—
Vom Himmel kam der Engel Schar 607*	OB9	25/2:10	7:12	1:14	5:54	7:10
Wachet auf, ruft uns die Stimme 645**	S1	25/2:63	8:100	1:86	7:72	8:2
Was fürchtst du Feind Heródes, sehr 696 (see Christum wir sollen 696)						
Wer nur den lieben Gott lässt walten 642*	OB43	25/2:58	7:64	1:72	5:57	7:58
Wer nur den lieben Gott 647**	S3	25/2:68	8:108	1:92	7:76	8:6
Wer nur den lieben Gott 690/1 (man.)		40:3	9:120	3:98	5:56/2	6:96
[chorale] 690/2		40:3	9:121	3:99	5:57	6:18

Composition

Composition	Coll.	Modern Editions				
		BGA	Lo	NBA	Pe	WS
Wer nur den lieben Gott 691*		40:4	9:122	3:98	5:56/1	6:97
(691a; by JSB?)		40:151	9:154		5:111	—
Wie schön leuchtet der Morgenstern 739*		40:99	9:123		9:56	6:98
Wie schön leuchtet 763 (not by JSB)		—	—			—
Wie schön leuchtet [incomplete] 764*		40:164	—		(K:49)	6:102
Wir glauben all' an einen Gott 680**	C12	3:212	8:44	4:52	7:78	7:86
Wir glauben 681** (man.)	C13	3:216	8:48	4:57	7:81	7:89
Wir glauben 740 (Johann Ludwig Krebs?)		40:103	9:133		7:82	6:121
Wir glauben 765 (not by JSB)		40:187	9:131		9:62	6:120+
Wir glauben 1098 (ME = N:20)		—	—		—	—

1. *The Diapason* 76 (June 1985): 9–13, with revisions for this Appendix by William Bates. Used by permission. No other reproduction of this material is permitted.

2. See, for example, *Allein Gott* 662 and 662a. In Lo the revised version (BWV 662) is printed in normal type, whereas different readings in the earlier version (BWV 662a) are printed as alternate notations.

3. In Lo part of *Allein Gott* 663a appears on p. V.

4. Presumably because *Jesu, meine Freude* 753 forms part of the *Clavier- Büchlein für Wilhelm Friedemann Bach*, the editors of the NBA include the piece in series V (Harpsicord/Lute Works 5:8) rather than in series IV.

5. The Lo printing of *Nun danket* includes only a few of the readings that differentiate BWV 657a from BWV 657.

6. In Lo part of *Nun komm'* 661a appears on p. VII.

7. Because its opening subject is essentially identical to the first phrase of the hymn tune "St. Anne," the Fugue in E flat (BWV 552/2) is listed in this Appendix among the chorale-based works.

52